The Numb

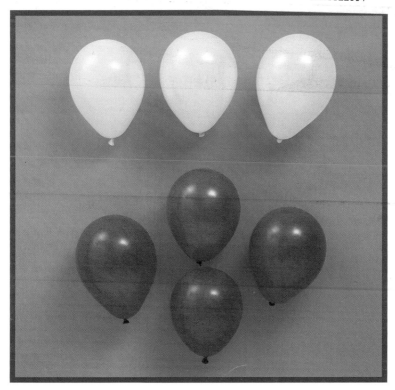

Adria Klein

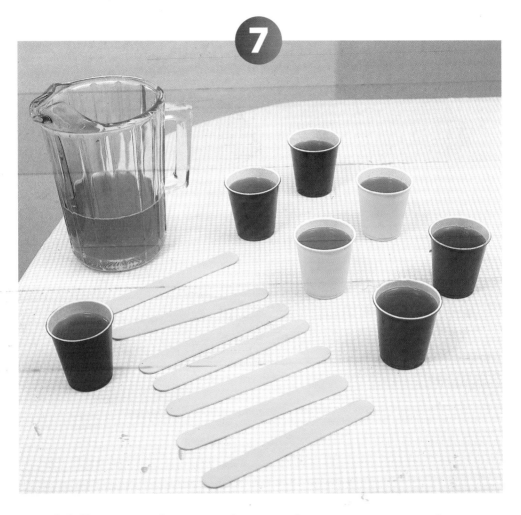

What does it take to make

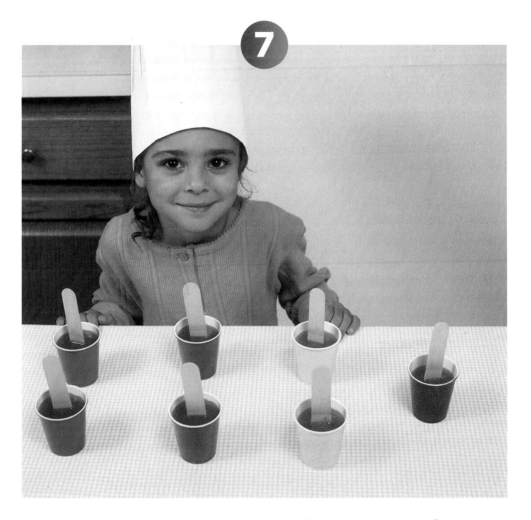

seven yummy ice pops?

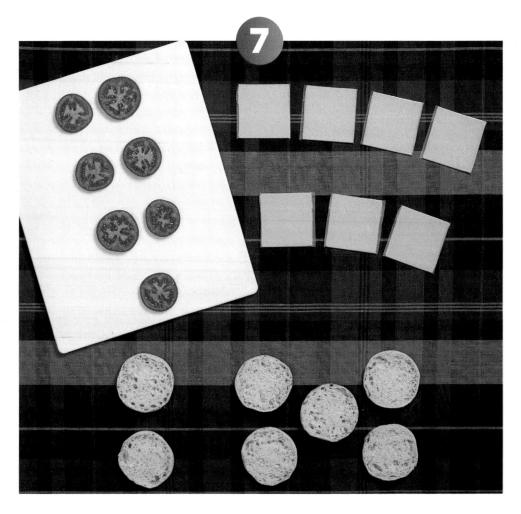

What does it take to make

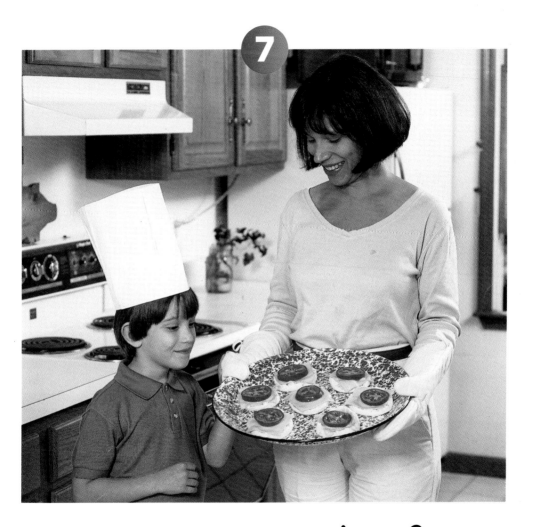

seven yummy pizzas?

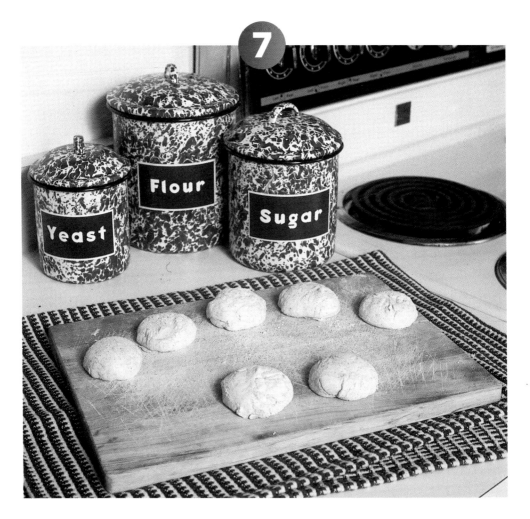

What does it take to make

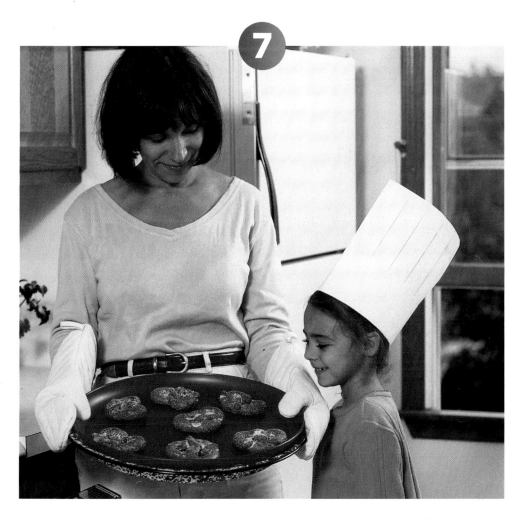

seven yummy pretzels?

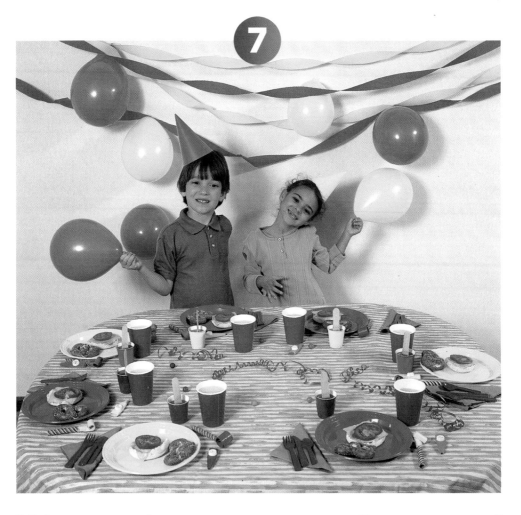

We can have a party for seven!